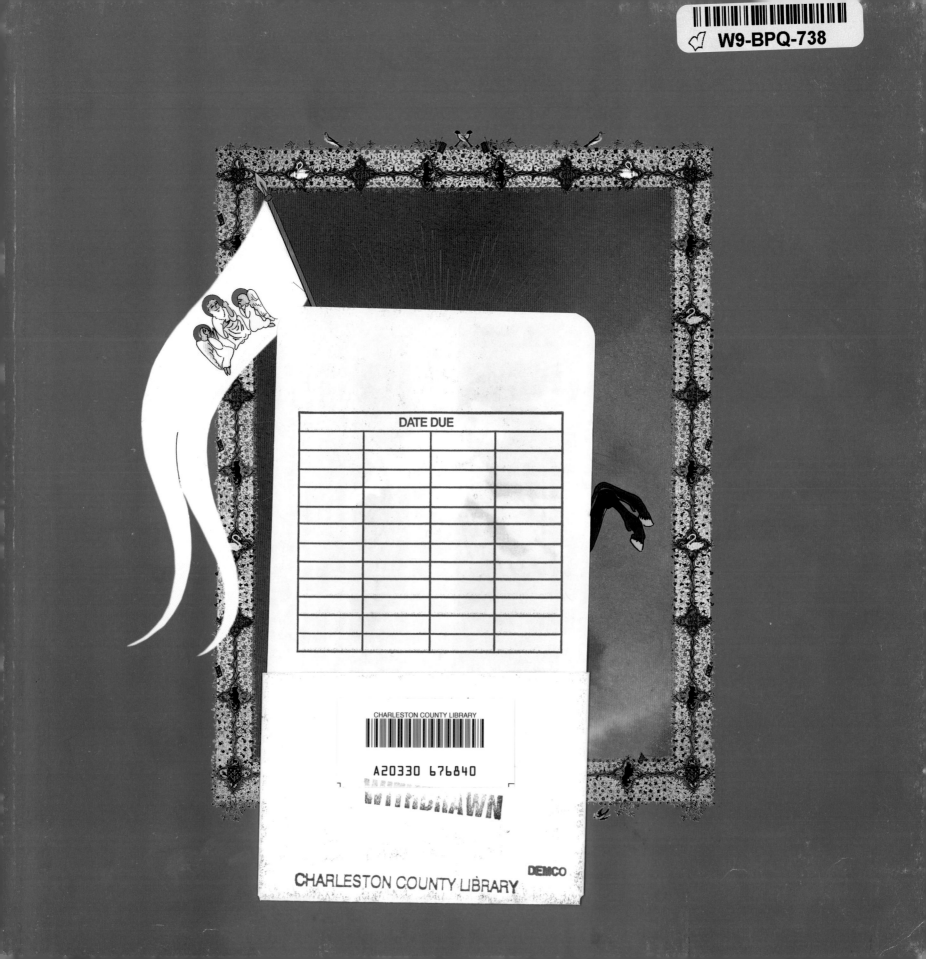

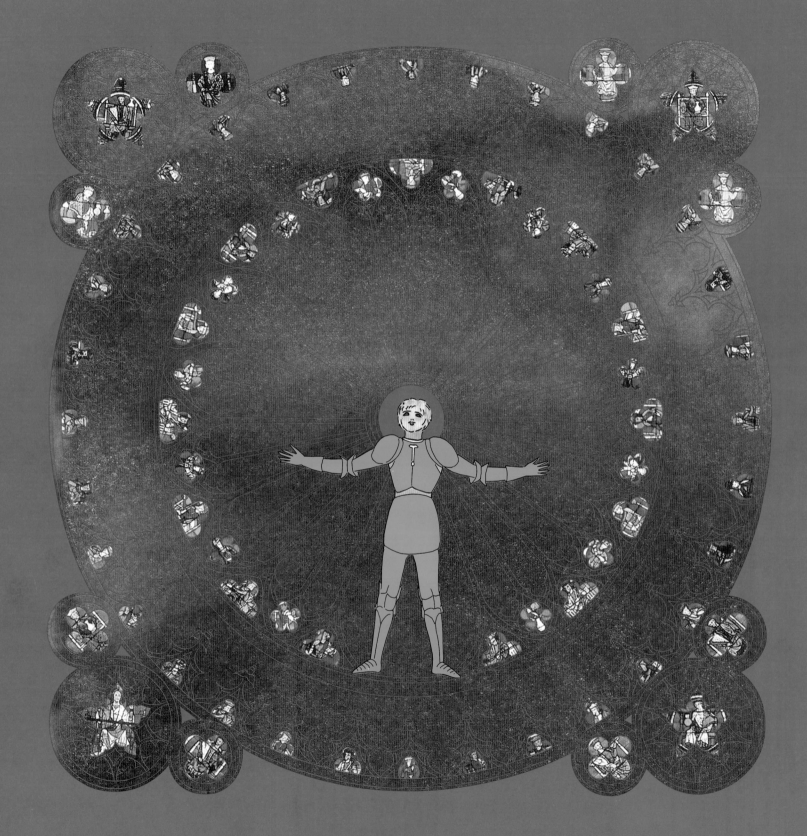

JOAN OF ARC

written and illustrated

by

DEMI

MARSHALL CAVENDISH CHILDREN

A NOTE FROM DEMI

For background material on Joan of Arc, I studied the exquisite medieval art of the fifteenth century: illuminated manuscripts, stained glass, architecture, painting and sculpture. Of most importance were *The Grandes Heures of Jean, Duke of Berry* (New York: Thames and Hudson, 1958); *The Belles Heures of Jean, Duke of Berry, Prince of France* (New York: George Braziller, 1977); *The Très Riches Heures of Jean, Duke of Berry* (New York: George Braziller, 2008); *The Bedford Hours: The Making of a Medieval Masterpiece* (London: British Library, 2007); *The Prayer Book of Charles the Bold: A Study of a Flemish Masterpiece from the Burgundian Court* (Los Angeles: Getty Publications, 2008); and *The Hours of Jeanne d'Evreux: A Prayer Book for a Queen* (New York: Metropolitan Museum of Art, 1999). I was also inspired by *A Thousand Years of Stained Glass*, by Catherine Brisac (New York: DK Publishing, 1994); *Architecture of Truth*, by Lucien Hervé, prefaced by Le Corbusier (New York: Phaidon Press, 2001); and *Art and Beauty in the Middle Ages*, by Umberto Eco (New Haven: Yale University Press, 2002). I read all the children's books on Saint Joan, including titles by Andrew Lang, Mark Twain, and Maurice Boutet de Monvel, and studied the art of Henry J. Ford, Howard Pyle and J. Jellicoe. For the text, the most inspirational book was *Joan of Arc by Herself and Her Witnesses*, by Régine Pernoud, translated from the French by Edward Hyams (Lanham, MD: Scarborough House, 1982).

Marshall Cavendish Corporation, 99 White Plains Road, Tarrytown, NY 10591
www.marshallcavendish.us/kids

Thanks to Brigitte Miriam Bedos-Rezak, Professor, Department of History, New York University, for her expert evaluation of the text and artwork.

LIBRARY OF CONGRESS CATALOGING-IN-PUBLICATION DATA:
Demi. Joan of Arc / by Demi. – 1st ed. p. cm.
ISBN 978-0-7614-5953-8 (hardcover) – ISBN 978-0-7614-5999-6 (ebook)
1. Joan, of Arc, Saint, 1412-1431–Juvenile literature. 2. France–History–Charles VII, 1422-1461–Juvenile literature. 3. Christian saints–France–Biography–Juvenile literature. I. Title. DC103.5.D46 2011 944'.026092–dc22 [B] 2011001123

The illustrations are rendered in mixed media.
Book design by Michael Nelson
Editor: Margery Cuyler
Printed in China (E)
First edition
1 3 5 6 4 2

"One life is all we have and we live it as we believe in living it.
But to sacrifice what you are and to live without belief,
that is a fate more terrible than dying."
—Joan of Arc

JOAN OF ARC

was born on January 6, 1412, to Isabelle and Jacques d'Arc in Domrémy, France. Little did she know that one day she would be one of the greatest generals in the history of France.

Joan had three brothers and one sister. She learned to spin and sew, and she loved the sound of church bells and the music and singing in church. Often she would go off by herself to pray in the fields and to feel the presence of God. From a very early age, Joan began to care for the sick and give money to the poor; she was a great help and comfort to all.

But life was very dangerous. France was at war with Burgundy and England. Each wanted to ascend the throne of France. The English and Burgundians were killing French people, burning their homes, and stealing their livestock.

With all the warfare, Dauphin Charles of France did not have the courage to lead France to victory. He did not have the courage to go to Reims Cathedral to get himself crowned king. Instead he stayed in his palace at Chinon and thought about his own escape.

As a young girl, Joan deeply felt the injustice of the invaders, and she fervently prayed for the deliverance of France. "God is good and just and right. Surely there will be justice!"

One summer day, when Joan was thirteen, she went to pray in her father's garden, and she saw a great light, dazzling and brilliant. From that light, there came the voice and appearance of Archangel Michael, who told her that it was she who would save the kingdom of France, who would go to the dauphin Charles and lead him to Reims Cathedral to be crowned king. Joan fell to her knees and said, "I am so young and powerless and do not know how to ride a horse or lead a war!"

"God will help you!" replied the archangel.

Then, instinctively, Joan knew he had been sent to her by God.

From that day on, Joan prayed devoutly. She saw angels and heard their voices, and she learned the language of the saints. Many times they told her of her mission to save France. Then one day in 1428, when Joan was sixteen, Saint Catherine and Saint Margaret appeared to her and announced that she must go at once to visit the dauphin Charles.

"As God has commanded it, it has to be!" said Joan. She then sought the help of Sire Robert of Baudricourt, Lord of Vaucouleurs. Joan said, "I have come before you from my Lord who wishes the dauphin to be made King, and it is I who will take him to be crowned!"

"Who is your Lord?" Baudricourt asked.

"The King of Heaven!" Joan replied.

"She is crazy! Box her ears and take her home!" yelled Baudricourt, and so Joan returned in shame to Domrémy.

Joan did not give up. She went back to Baudricourt two more times with urgent news from her voices. "The dauphin is being besieged at Orléans!" she told him. "I must help him! God has willed this and I was born to do this." Calling herself the Maid of God, finally she persuaded Baudricourt to grant her some soldiers to escort her to the dauphin. The people of Vaucouleurs gave her a suit of armor, a horse, and a sword. Everyone prayed that God would watch over her on her journey.

The English and Burgundians were everywhere. Joan had to travel by night and keep herself hidden by day. Her escorts began to lose heart and wanted to turn back, but Joan answered, "Fear nothing, for God is leading me!"

The court of Dauphin
Charles could not agree on
whether to receive Joan.
Many urged the dauphin
not to see her at all.

But Orleáns was surrounded and about to fall to the English, and Joan was the dauphin's last hope of saving the city. So he had her admitted to his court.

Still suspicious, Dauphin Charles decided to test Joan to see if she really was inspired by God. He dressed in plain clothes and put one of his nobles on the throne to impersonate the king. By the light of flaring torches, Joan entered the throne room.

Joan had never seen Dauphin Charles before, but immediately her voices helped her single him out. Kneeling before him, she said, "Very noble Lord Dauphin, I am come and am sent by God to bring help to you and your kingdom, to raise the siege of Orléans, and to crown you king!"

Still the cowardly dauphin hesitated. Fearing Joan might be an evil sorceress, he sent her to be examined by learned and powerful churchmen. For three weeks, Joan boldly answered every question with great clarity and self-control. Swayed by Joan's faith, the churchmen finally agreed to accept her as their military leader.

Amidst great cheering crowds, Joan rode to meet the French forces at Blois. Commander Dunois greeted her, and Joan said to him, "I bring you the best of help, that of the King of Heaven! It comes not from me, but from God Himself!"

Joan's great confidence inspired everyone, and soon the battle for Orléans began. "Nothing is impossible with the power of God!" Joan yelled from the center of the fight. With her banner that said "Jesus, Maria" raised high, she gave great courage and hope to all the soldiers.

Commander Dunois was jealous of Joan and wanted to grab victory for himself. Once during the battle, he ordered an attack on a bastion while Joan was resting. But the attack failed, and Dunois' French troops retreated in great disarray until Joan rushed to their rescue. Rallying the fleeing men, she forced the English to surrender and was led in great glory back to Orléans. After four days, the English, who had been fighting for eight months in Orléans, gave up the siege and withdrew.

Often Joan disagreed with her commanders' worldly advice and military tactics because she was listening to her voices and angels. Certain that she had heard the truth from the Voice of God, she led her men with spirit and resolve and inspired them with boundless faith.

As news of the victory of Orléans spread far and wide, the French came to believe that Joan was led by God. Never stopping a moment for praise, Joan quickly went to Dauphin Charles to arrange his coronation in Reims Cathedral.

But the dauphin refused to go, because he did not want his easy life and royal existence disturbed.

Joan, who wanted to act swiftly, was frustrated by the dauphin's hesitation. Rallying the French around her, she went back to fighting the English. She won the battles of Jargeau, Meung, Beaugency, Patay, and Troyes.

Finally, but still reluctantly, Charles agreed to go to Reims for his coronation. On July 17, 1429, the dauphin's procession made its way through cheering crowds and joyous music to the cathedral.

In the cathedral, Joan stood next to Charles, proudly carrying her banner, which she said "had borne the burden and deserved the honor." She knelt before the king and wept. "O king, now is accomplished the will of God!"

All who saw her at this moment believed she was truly an instrument of God. After the ceremony, the people fought to kiss her hands and clothes or just to touch her. This was Joan's greatest moment of triumph.

Now that Joan had obeyed the commands that God had given her, she earnestly asked the king to let her return to her home in Domrémy. In all that she did, she had never thought of reward or self-glorification but only of simple devotion to God, country, and king. Charles VII would not let her go, however. He ordered her to remain in command of the royal army.

At this command, a great indecision came upon Joan. Against her better judgment, she obeyed the king's voice and not her inner voices. As soon as she did this, her voices deserted her, her saints and angels fled, and she felt defeated.

Still Joan wanted to help the king and win back Paris for the French. But the king was slow to act, and so the English had plenty of time to build their defenses. Finally the king decided to allow Joan to lead a small band of soldiers to fight the enemy northeast of Paris.

However, Joan and her men were driven back, and Joan was severely wounded in the thigh. She had to be dragged away from the ramparts and forced to abandon the fight.

This was Joan's first defeat, and immediately the French began to doubt her powers. They wondered if God was still on her side. "One sent by God," they said, "could never be defeated!" They did not realize that after the coronation, Joan had followed the king's will and not the will of God. When King Charles VII heard of the defeat near Paris, he refused to allow Joan to launch any further attacks. With her heart full of grief, Joan followed the king's orders.

King Charles VII disbanded
his army and stopped
attacking the English
and Burgundians.

Joan was in despair. She left the king and went to help the heroic, scattered bands of Frenchmen still fighting the English. Joan managed to capture Saint-Pierre-le-Moutier and tried to besiege La Charité-sur-Loire, but because she received no funds or supplies from King Charles VII, she was forced to retreat.

Next she went to
Compiègne to help a
French garrison fight the
English and Burgundians
there. Again Joan and her
army had to retreat . . .

. . . for when they came to the walls of Compiègne, they found the gates were shut. The French commander, whom Joan had come to assist, had shut her out. Joan defended herself until a troop of Burgundians rushed upon her. Even then she did not surrender but was forcibly dragged off her horse. From the walls of the city, the French governor saw her taken prisoner but did not raise a finger to save her.

With her back against the bank of the moat, Joan fell into the hands of her enemies, the Burgundians. They sold her to the English, and King Charles VII of France, whom Joan had set on the throne, never even offered a ransom.

Shut up in a dungeon at Rouen, Joan was guarded night and day by soldiers and forced to endure their brutality. On February 21, 1431, at age nineteen, Joan's trial began. She stood before forty-four men who questioned her Catholic faith. She answered all their questions with a purity of heart.

Finally Joan was taken to a cemetery, where her death sentence was read to her. She was condemned for wearing men's clothes and told she would be burned at the stake unless she confessed. If she confessed, her sentence would be changed to life imprisonment.

In a moment of extreme
weakness and exhaustion,
Joan signed the confession.

Almost immediately Joan repented the confession. She declared that her statement was false and that she would rather die than deny that all she had done had been with the help of God alone.

Having spoken the truth and cleansed her soul, Joan began hearing her voices again and was comforted in knowing that God was at her side.

In the marketplace at Rouen, Joan was led to her execution. She was chained to the stake, and as flames blazed around her, she was heard to call out many times, "Jesus! Jesus! Jesus!"

Everyone around her wept, even the judges and executioners. One said, "We are all lost for we have burned a saint!"

The cruel death of Joan
of Arc moved the French
people to rise up in fury
and drive the English out of
their country. Joan had died
at the stake, but she would
live forever, for she had
made a nation of France.
Twenty-six years later,
the Catholic Church held
a new trial, where Joan
was declared innocent. She
was canonized as a saint in
1920 and today is honored
as a patron saint of France.

ENGLAND

London

English Channel

Rouen • Compìcane
Reims
Marne River *Metz River*
Paris • Vaucouleurs
Domrémy

Seine River

Loire River Orléans
Jargeau
Chinon
Fierbois *Burgundy*

*Atlantic
Ocean*
Poitiers

FRANCE

Rhine River

Rhone River

Mediterranean Sea

Fifteenth Century France

SILVER – LAND HELD BY ENGLAND AND BURGUNDY
GOLD – LAND HELD BY KING CHARLES VII

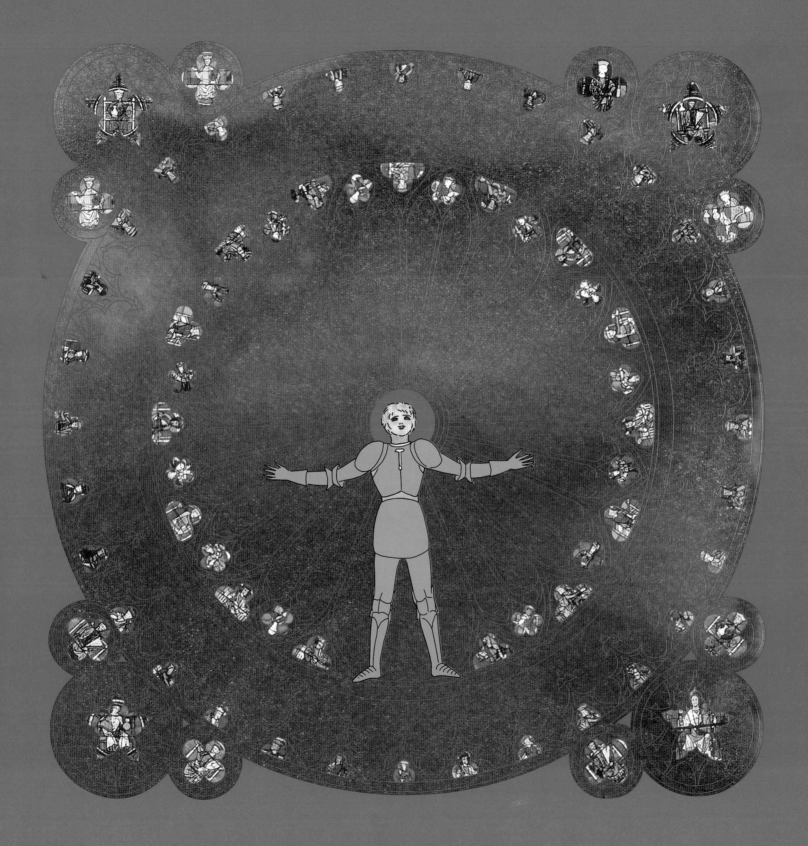